Kingdom Kidz Bible

with envelope surprises!

Zacchaeus

Zacchaeus: Luke 19:1–9

PROMISE
PRESS

An Imprint of Barbour Publishing

W atch out for Zacchaeus, a man whispered to his wife. "He cheated on taxes and stole our money." Zacchaeus frowned. His heart was cold and hard. He didn't care what people said.

Someone shouted, "Here comes Jesus!"

"Let me see Him!" Zacchaeus cried, pushing his way through the crowd. But no one paid attention to short Zacchaeus. They wanted to see Jesus, too.

Zacchaeus had an idea. He spotted a sycamore tree near the road. Grabbing the lowest branch in his hands, he pulled himself up and started to climb the tree.

Up, up, up. Zacchaeus climbed until he reached a branch above the people's heads. "There's Jesus!" he shouted. "I see Him!"

Jesus walked down the road. He stopped right under the
sycamore tree. What a surprise!

"Climb down here, Zacchaeus," Jesus said. "I'm
coming to your house today."

Zacchaeus slid down, down, down the tree. Bump! He landed on the ground. Standing up, he looked at Jesus. Suddenly, Zacchaeus felt his heart change. The love Jesus showed him made him feel full of joy. Zacchaeus now knew Jesus was really God's Son. He knew Jesus wanted him to do good things and not bad.

Lord, Zacchaeus said, "right now I'll give half my money to the poor. Plus, I'll pay back the people I cheated!" Jesus looked straight at Zacchaeus and smiled. Jesus knew Zacchaeus's heart had changed. "Today you are saved," He said. "You will live forever in heaven with Me!"

I know Jesus is actually God's Son. Today I pray,
Dear Jesus, I *know* You and I *love* You! Amen.